W9-CMJ-627

Discarded

Make and Eat

Cookies
and Cakes

Susannah Blake

PowerKiDS
press.

New York

Published in 2009 by The Rosen Publishing Group Inc.
29 East 21st Street, New York, NY 10010

First Edition

Senior editor: Jennifer Schofield
Designer: Jane Hawkins
Photographer: Andy Crawford
Proofreader: Susie Brooks

Library of Congress Cataloging-in-Publication Data

Blake, Susannah.
   Cookies and cakes / Susannah Blake. — 1st ed.
      p. cm. — (Make and eat)
   Includes index.
   ISBN 978-1-4358-2859-9 (lib. binding)
   ISBN 978-1-4358-2933-6 (paperback)
   ISBN 978-1-4358-2937-4 (6-pack)
   1. Cookies—Juvenile literature. 2. Cake—Juvenile literature. I. Title.
   TX772.B5736 2009
   641.8'654—dc22

                                        2008025804

Manufactured in China

The author and publisher would like to thank the following models:
Adam Menditta, Harriet Couch, Demi Mensah, Robert Kilminster,
Aneesa Qureshi, Kaine Zachary Levy, Emel Augustin,
Claire Shanahan.
All photographs by Andy Crawford except page 4: Kevin Fleming/
Corbis; page 5 Marie Dubrac/ANYONE/Getty images

Web Sites

Due to the changing nature of Internet links,
PowerKids Press has developed an online list of Web
sites related to the subject of this book. This site is
updated regularly. Please use this link to access this list:
www.powerkidslinks.com/mae/ccakes

Note to parents and teachers:

The recipes in this book are intended
to be made by children. However, we
recommend adult supervision at all times,
especially when using kitchen equipment,
since the Publisher cannot be held
responsible for any injury.

Contents

All about cookies and cakes

There are many kinds of cookie and cake. They can have different tastes, textures, colors, and shapes depending on the ingredients used. Often they are sweet, but they can be savory, too. Most cookies and cakes are baked in the oven, but some do not need baking and are chilled in the refrigerator instead.

DIFFERENT KINDS OF COOKIE AND CAKE

Butter, sugar, eggs, and flour are the main ingredients used to make cookies and cakes. But you can add other ingredients, such as oats, corn syrup, dried fruit, chocolate, and nuts. The way you combine and bake these ingredients can give amazing results. Different combinations will produce different kinds of cookie and cake. Some will be soft and chewy, some will be crisp and crumbly, and others will be light and airy.

BAKING PANS AND COOKIE SHEETS

Cakes and cookies are usually baked in some kind of pan or case. For example, little paper cases can be used to make cupcakes (see right) or if you are making a large cake, you would use layer cake pans, which are perfect for stacking one cake on top of another. Cookies are often baked on cookie sheets—these are metal pans that can go in the oven.

DIFFERENT DECORATIONS

Most cookies and cakes can be served plain—but they can be decorated, too. This not only looks pretty and tastes good, but it can also be great fun! You can decorate cakes and cookies before baking. Try sprinkling flaked nuts or sugar on top of cakes or soft cookie doughs. Or you can press nuts or candied fruit on top.

Some people prefer to decorate cakes and cookies once they have been baked. Simple glazes or butter frostings are easy to make (see page 12–13) and can be spooned or spread on top of a baked cake or cookie. If you like, you can add more decorations. Pretty colored candies, sprinkles, and fruit and nuts all look good. You could also add a dusting of confectioners' sugar to cakes.

GET STARTED!

In this book, you can learn to make all kinds of cookie and cake. All the recipes use everyday kitchen equipment, such as knives, spoons, forks, and cutting boards. You can see pictures of the different equipment that you may need on page 23. Before you start, check that you have all the equipment that you will need and make a list of any ingredients you need to buy. Also check that there is an adult to help you, especially with the recipes that involve using the stove or oven.

When you have everything you need, make sure all the kitchen surfaces are clean, and wash your hands well with soap and water. If you have long hair, tie it back. Always wash raw fruits and vegetables under cold running water before preparing or cooking them. Then, put on an apron and get baking!

Fruity oat bars

These chewy oat bars make a great treat to add to your lunchbox. The oat bars will look soft when you take them out of the oven, but they get harder as they cool.

INGREDIENTS

For 16 oat bars:
- 1 stick + 1 tbsp butter, plus extra for greasing
- 3 oz. (75g) dried apricots
- ½ cup sugar
- 5 tbsp light corn syrup
- 2 cups rolled oats
- 2 tbsp sunflower seeds
- 2 tbsp pumpkin seeds

EXTRA EQUIPMENT

8 in. x 8 in. (20cm x 20cm) cake pan

Ask an adult to help you use the stove and oven.

1 Preheat the oven to 350°F (180°C). Grease the cake pan with butter, making sure the base and sides are coated all over.

ROLLED OATS

Oats are a type of cereal that grow well in moist, cool climates. The grains are steamed and flattened to make rolled oats. In many countries, rolled oats are cooked and eaten hot as oatmeal, or mixed with fruit and seeds to make crunchy granola.

2 Roughly chop the apricots and set them aside for later.

3 Put the butter, sugar, and corn syrup in a pan and set it over very low heat. Stir now and then, until the butter has melted.

6

4 When the butter has melted, remove the pan from the heat and stir the dough well. Add the oats, seeds, and apricots and stir again.

5 Pour the dough into the pan and spread it out in an even layer. Make sure you push the dough up into the corners of the pan.

6 Bake for about 25 minutes until golden. Wearing a pair of oven gloves, take the pan out of the oven and put it on a heatproof surface.

7 Leave the oat bar to cool in the pan. When cool, cut into quarters. Then cut each quarter into four squares to make a total of 16 squares.

Chocolate chip cookies

These simple cookies, made with creamed butter and sugar, are a real classic. The soft dough needs no shaping and can simply be dropped onto cookie sheets in big dollops.

INGREDIENTS

For 20 cookies:
- 1 stick butter, at room temperature, plus extra for greasing
- ⅓ cup sugar • 1 egg, lightly beaten
- 1 tsp vanilla extract
- 1⅓ cups all-purpose flour
- ½ tsp baking powder
- 3½ oz. (100g) chocolate chips

EXTRA EQUIPMENT

- 3 cookie sheets • sieve • wire rack

Ask an adult to help you use the oven.

1 Preheat the oven to 375°F (190°C). Grease the cookie sheets with butter.

2 Put the butter and sugar in a bowl, and beat them together with a wooden spoon until they are smooth and creamy.

3 Gradually add the egg to the creamed ingredients and beat well. Add the vanilla extract and beat until everything is mixed together.

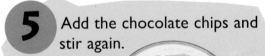

4 Put the flour and baking powder in a clean bowl and mix them together. Sieve the flour into the creamed ingredients, and stir until creamy and well blended.

5 Add the chocolate chips and stir again.

6 Use a teaspoon to scoop up heaped spoonfuls of the dough. Using another teaspoon, scrape the dough onto the cookie sheets. Space the blobs of cookie dough well apart to allow them to spread during baking. You should end up with about eight blobs of dough on each cookie sheet.

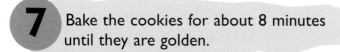

7 Bake the cookies for about 8 minutes until they are golden.

8 Using a pair of oven gloves, take the cookie sheets out of the oven and put them on a heatproof surface. Allow the cookies to harden for about 1 minute. When hard, transfer the cookies to a wire rack to cool.

MAKING CAKES AND COOKIES RISE

Baking powder is a raising agent used to make cakes and cookies rise. It is made from an alkali ingredient (baking soda) and an acidic ingredient (cream of tartar). When these two ingredients come into contact with a wet ingredient, they react to make carbon dioxide. The carbon dioxide makes tiny bubbles in cake batter or cookie dough, which cause it to rise.

Cheesy cookies

These savory cookies are flavored with tangy Cheddar cheese. When you want a treat, they make a great alternative to a traditional sweet cookie.

INGREDIENTS

For 15 cookies:
- 1 stick butter, at room temperature, plus extra for greasing
- 4½ oz. (115g) Cheddar cheese
- black pepper
- 1⅓ cups self-rising flour • cold water

EXTRA EQUIPMENT

- 2 cookie sheets • sieve
- wire rack

Ask an adult to help you use the oven.

1 Preheat the oven to 350°F (180°C). Grease two cookie sheets with butter, making sure the surface is coated all over.

2 Grate the cheese.

3 Put the butter and cheese in a bowl and add freshly ground black pepper. Beat them together until they make a soft, creamy mixture.

4 Sieve the flour into the cheese mixture. Stir the dough together and then bring it together with your hands.

5 Break off walnut-sized lumps of dough and roll them between your hands to make round balls. Place them on the cookie sheets, spacing them wide apart.

6 Dip a fork into cold water, then gently press the top of each ball to flatten it. You will need to keep dipping the fork in water to stop it from sticking to the cookie dough.

7 Bake the cookies for 15–20 minutes until they are golden brown.

8 Using a pair of oven gloves, take the cookie sheets out of the oven and put them on a heatproof surface. Allow the cookies to cool for a minute, then use a metal spatula to transfer to a wire rack to cool.

COOLING COOKIES

Most cookies need to be moved to a wire rack to cool soon after baking. This allows cool air to circulate all around the cookie, making sure it stays crisp. If the cookie was left on the cookie sheet, condensation (or moisture) would make the cookie soggy.

Victoria layer cake

This cake is made using a classic cake batter. It uses equal weights of butter, sugar, eggs, and flour. It is one of the easiest and most tasty layer cakes to make.

INGREDIENTS

For 1 layer cake:

- 1½ sticks butter, at room temperature, plus extra for greasing
- ¾ cup sugar • 3 eggs
- 1½ cups self-rising flour
- 4 tbsp strawberry jam
- 1 tbsp confectioners' sugar

EXTRA EQUIPMENT

- baking parchment • 2 8 in. (20cm) layer cake pans • pencil • scissors • 2 wire racks

Ask an adult to help you use the oven

1 Preheat the oven to 350°F (180°C).

2 Cut off enough baking parchment to cover both layer cake pans. Place one of the pans on the edge of the paper and draw around it to make a circle. Repeat to make a second circle. Cut out the circles and check that they fit inside the pans. Set them aside.

3 Grease the inside of each pan with butter, then slip a paper circle into the base of each pan and press it down flat.

4 Put the butter and sugar in a bowl and beat them until they are smooth and creamy. Break one egg into the mixture and beat it well. Beat in another egg, then add the last egg and beat once again.

5 Sieve the flour over the butter mixture, then stir it gently until the batter is creamy.

6 Spoon half of the batter into one pan and spread it out with the back of the spoon. Spoon the remaining batter into the second pan and spread it out.

HOW TO CRACK AN EGG

1. Hold the egg in one hand and knock the middle on the side of a bowl to make a deep crack in its shell.

2. Holding the egg over the bowl, put your thumbs into the crack.

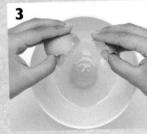

3. Pull the halves apart so that the egg falls into the bowl. Check that no pieces of shell fell into the bowl.

7 Bake for 20–25 minutes until each cake is golden and risen. To test if the cake is baked, poke a skewer into the center—it should come out clean. If the cake sticks to the skewer, then put the cake back into the oven for a few more minutes.

8 Use oven gloves to take the cakes out of the oven and put them on a heatproof surface. Ask an adult to help you to transfer the cakes to wire racks. Peel off the baking parchment and allow the cakes to cool.

9 When cool, put one cake the right way up on a plate. Ask an adult to help you slice a thin layer off the top of the cake to give it a flat surface. Spread the top with jam, then place the second cake on top.

10 Put the confectioners' sugar in a sieve and hold it over the cake. Tap the side until the top of the cake is dusted with a layer of sugar.

13

Banana and fig muffins

Muffins are great for a weekend breakfast or brunch, or an after-school treat with a glass of milk. They are best eaten on the day you make them—that is why this recipe makes only six at a time.

INGREDIENTS

For 6 muffins:
- 3 tbsp butter
- 1 cup + 1 tbsp self-rising flour
- ½ tsp baking powder
- ¼ tsp baking soda
- 2 tbsp sugar
- 1 large ripe banana, peeled
- 1 egg • ¼ cup milk
- 4 dried figs

EXTRA EQUIPMENT

- 6-hole muffin pan • 6 paper muffin cups
- sieve • wire rack

Ask an adult to help you use the oven.

1 Preheat the oven to 375°F (190°C). Put a paper muffin cup inside each hole in the muffin pan.

2 Put the butter in a small pan and warm it over low heat until it is melted. Set it aside.

3 Sieve the flour, baking powder, baking soda, and sugar into a bowl. Make a well in the middle of the ingredients.

4 Mash the banana. Add the egg, milk, and melted butter to the banana and stir together until it is well mixed.

5 Cut the woody steams off the figs. Roughly chop the figs and add them to the banana mixture. Stir the mixture well.

DRIED FRUIT

Drying fruit preserves it and allows it to keep much longer than fresh fruit. Fruit can be dried by heat from the Sun or in a machine called a *dehydrator*. Drying fruit changes the texture and taste of the fruit, making it taste much stronger and sweeter.

6 Pour the banana mixture into the well in the dry ingredients. Mix all the ingredients together until they are just combined. Do not mix too much, because the batter needs to have a rough texture.

7 Using a tablespoon, spoon the muffin batter into the paper cups. Bake for 20 minutes until the muffins are risen and golden.

8 Wearing a pair of oven gloves, carefully take the muffin pan out of the oven and put it on a heatproof surface. Using a clean towel to protect your hands, lift the muffins out of the pan and transfer them to a wire rack to cool. Serve warm or cold.

Candy cookies

These pretty cookies are fun to make and delicious to eat. You can be as creative as you like when it comes to decorating them. Spread a smooth layer of frosting on each cookie, then decorate them with bright-colored candies.

INGREDIENTS

For 25–30 cookies:
- 1½ sticks butter, chilled, plus extra for greasing
- 2 cups all-purpose flour, plus extra for dusting
- ½ cup sugar • 1 egg yolk

For the frosting:
- 2 tbsp lemon juice
- 1¾ cup confectioners' sugar, sifted
- small candies to decorate

EXTRA EQUIPMENT

- food processor • plastic wrap
- rolling pin • 2½ in. (6cm) cookie cutter
- cookie sheets • metal spatula

Ask an adult to help you use the oven.

1 Cut the butter into small cubes.

2 Put the flour in a food processor and put the chilled butter on top of it. Turn on the food processor in short bursts until the mixture looks like fine breadcrumbs.

3 Add the egg yolk and sugar to the food processor, and process until the dough comes together in a ball.

4 Sprinkle a little flour on your work surface, then knead the dough until it is smooth. Shape it into a ball and wrap it in plastic wrap. Put it in the refrigerator for at least 30 minutes to harden.

SEPARATING EGGS

Some recipes call for just the yolk or just the white of an egg. To separate an egg, crack it against the edge of a bowl so that there is a deep crack in the shell. Put your fingers in the crack and pull the shell apart. Keep the yolk in one half of the shell and let the white fall into the bowl. Throw away the part of the egg that you do not need or keep it for another recipe.

5 Preheat the oven to 350°F (180°C). Grease two cookie sheets with butter.

6 Sprinkle a light layer of flour on your work surface, then put the ball of chilled dough on top and sprinkle it with a little more flour. Using a rolling pin, roll dough out to a thin layer.

7 Using the cookie cutter, cut out circles from the dough, cutting as closely together as you can. Transfer the circles to the cookie sheets, spacing them slightly apart.

8 Bake the cookies for about 12 minutes until they are pale golden. Then use a pair of oven gloves to take the cookie sheets out of the oven and put them on a heatproof surface. Slide a metal spatula underneath and transfer the cookies to the wire rack to cool.

9 To make the frosting, put the lemon juice in a bowl and gradually stir in the confectioners' sugar until it looks smooth and creamy.

10 Spread the frosting on the cookies and decorate them with colored candies.

Marshmallow fingers

These rich, squashy bars are easy to make and require no baking. Instead, just chill them in the refrigerator.

INGREDIENTS

For 8 squares:
- 1¾ oz. (45g) brazil nuts
- 3 oz. (85g) ginger snaps
- 6 oz. (150g) milk chocolate
- 1 tbsp butter
- 1¾ oz. (45g) mini marshmallows
- confectioners' sugar for dusting

EXTRA EQUIPMENT
- plastic wrap • 2 lb. loaf pan
- plastic bag • rolling pin • sieve

Ask an adult to help you use the stove.

1 Tear off a piece of plastic wrap, wider and longer than the loaf pan, and lay it on top of the pan. Press it down so that it covers the base of the pan. Let the extra plastic wrap hang over the edges.

2 Put the nuts on a board and chop each one in half to use later.

3 Put the ginger snaps in a plastic bag and twist the top of the bag to seal it. Hold the twisted top of the bag in one hand, and use a rolling pin to tap the cookies to break them up into small pieces. Do not hit them too much or you will end up with just crumbs. If you have a few big pieces of cookie left in the bag, break these up with your fingers.
Set the cookies aside.

4 Pour water into a pan so that it is about 1½ in. (4cm) deep. Rest a bowl inside the pan so it hangs above, but does not touch the water. Put the pan on medium heat and let the water boil. Then turn the heat as low as it will go, so that the water just simmers.

SOLID CHOCOLATE

Chocolate is a solid, but it can be melted and changed into a liquid. When the runny chocolate is cooled, it hardens to become a solid again. This type of change is called a *reversible change*, because it can continue to happen.

5 Break the chocolate into pieces and put it in the bowl with the butter. Wait until it is almost melted, then remove it from the heat and leave it to stand for a few minutes. Stir the chocolate until both the chocolate and butter are completely melted.

6 Add the nuts, cookies, and marshmallows to the chocolate and stir until they are well mixed.

7 Pour the batter into the pan and spread it out in an even layer, pressing down with a spoon. Fold the overhanging plastic wrap over the top so the dough is covered. Press down on the covered dough to make sure it is firmly packed in the pan.

8 Put the pan in the refrigerator for 2 hours until it is firm. Then turn the pan upside down so that the cake falls out. Unwrap the cake and place it on a cutting board.

9 Cut the cake into fingers. Dust the fingers with confectioners' sugar to serve.

Vanilla cupcakes

Cupcakes topped with creamy frosting are easy to make. You can choose whatever color you like for the frosting—yellow, pink, lilac, and green all look great.

INGREDIENTS

For 12 cupcakes:
- 1 stick butter, at room temperature
- ½ cup sugar   • 2 eggs
- ½ tsp vanilla extract
- 1 cup self-rising flour

For the icing:
- 5 tbsp butter   • 2 cups confectioners' sugar
- 2 tbsp milk   • ¼ tsp vanilla extract
- food coloring   • sprinkles

EXTRA EQUIPMENT

- 12-hole cupcake pan
- 12 paper cupcake cases   • sieve
- wire rack

Ask an adult to help you use the oven.

1 Preheat the oven to 350°F (180°C). Put a paper cupcake cup inside each hole in the cupcake pan.

2 Put the butter and sugar in a bowl and beat them to make a pale, creamy mixture.

3 Lightly beat the eggs and add them and the vanilla to the creamed butter a little at a time. Beat until it is smooth.

4 Sieve the flour into the butter mixture and stir until it makes a smooth, creamy batter.

5 Drop spoonfuls of the batter into the cupcake cups until you have divided the batter evenly between the cups.

6 Bake the cupcakes for 18 minutes until they are risen and golden. Wearing a pair of oven gloves, remove the pan from the oven and place it on a heatproof surface. After about a minute, transfer the cupcakes to a wire rack to cool.

7 When the cupcakes are cool, they are ready to decorate. Put the butter in a medium bowl and beat until it is creamy. Sieve the confectioners' sugar over the butter, and add the milk and vanilla. Stir until creamy. Add 1–2 drops of food coloring and mix well.

8 Spread the frosting on top of the cupcakes, then add sprinkles on top.

ARE THEY BAKED YET?

To check if your cupcakes are baked, gently press the top of one cake with the tip of your finger. If it is baked, the top will spring back. If it does not spring back, the cupcakes must go back in the oven for another minute or two.

Glossary

acid A substance that contains the gas hydrogen and causes chemical change. Cream of tartar is an acid.

alkali A substance that neutralizes (balances out) acids. Baking soda is an alkali.

candied fruit When fruit is preserved or stored in sugar, so that it has a glossy or shiny look.

carbon dioxide A colorless gas. Baking powder and self-rising flour produce tiny bubbles of carbon dioxide, which make cake batter and cookie dough rise in the oven.

circulate To move around and come back to the beginning.

coarse When something is rough.

glaze Frosting made from confectioners' sugar and water.

granola A cereal made from grains, nuts, and dried fruit.

kneading To press and stretch dough until it is soft and stretchy.

liquid A substance, such as water, that can flow but is not a gas.

reversible change A chemical change that can keep happening.

savory When flavors are tasty but not sweet. For example, cheese has a savory flavor.

solid A substance, such as wood, that keeps its shape.

texture The way the surface of something feels.

well A hollow or dip made in the middle of dry ingredients into which liquid is poured.

BOOKS TO READ

Kids Baking
by Abigail Johnson Dodge (Oxmoor House, 2003)

Just Desserts
by Marilyn Linton (Topeka Bindery, 2002)

MEASUREMENT CONVERSIONS

Liquid	Butter
1 cup = 8 fl. oz. (250 ml)	1 stick = 4 oz. (115g)
	1 tbsp = 1/2 oz. (15g)
Flour	
1 cup = 4 oz. (115g)	**Sugar**
1 tbsp = 1/2 oz. (15g)	1 cup = 9 oz. (225g)
	1 tbsp = 1 oz. (28g)

EXTRA INFORMATION

These abbreviations have been used:
• tbsp—tablespoon • tsp—teaspoon
• oz.—ounce • lb.—pound
• ml—milliliter • g—gram • l—liter

To work out where the stove dial needs to be for high, medium, and low heat, count the marks on the dial and divide it by three. The top few are high and the bottom few are low. The in-between ones are medium. All eggs are medium unless stated.

Equipment

PLASTIC SPATULA
These are great for scraping batter from the sides of bowls.

ROLLING PIN
Round, wooden rolling pins can be used to roll out cookie dough.

MEASURING SPOONS
Measuring spoons help you to use the exact amount of ingredients.

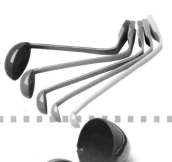

COOKIE CUTTERS
These come in many different shapes and sizes. Use them to cut out rolled dough.

MEASURING CUPS
These are used just like measuring spoons, but for measuring bigger quantities of ingredients.

BAKING PARCHMENT
Use to line baking pans and cake pans to prevent batter from sticking to the surface.

COOKIE SHEETS
Metal sheets for baking food in the oven.

PANS
These come in different sizes and are good for baking cupcakes and muffins.

SIEVE
These may be small, medium, or large and are useful for sifting flour and confectioners' sugar.

WIRE RACK
Cakes and cookies should always be cooled on a wire rack to allow air to circulate underneath.

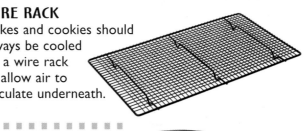

BAKING PANS
These come in all shapes and sizes so you can bake different shaped cakes.

FOOD SCALE
Use to measure dry and solid ingredients accurately.

Index